For Pria & Teddy,
And all other farm kids,
May you always stay safe on the farm.

ISBN: 9781763753273

First Edition

KEEP ME SAFE ON THE FARM

WRITTEN BY PIPPA BIRD
ILLUSTRATED BY PRIA BIRD

On this sprawling farm where adventures lie,
Keep me safe beneath the open sky.

From dawn until dusk, where the paddocks meet the light,
Let's journey together, keeping safety in sight.

With the tractor's roar and its mighty height,
Keep me clear of its path, day and night.

A powerful friend for the work we must do,
But respect its power and keep me in view.

Among the cows in the paddocks wide,
Stay cautious and calm by their gentle side.

They move with grace, but can startle too,
So keep me safe, steady, and always beside you.

By the dam where the water glistens bright,
Guard me well, keep me in your sight.

A tempting splash on a summer's day,
But safety first before we stomp and play.

Hay bales stacked high in a golden heap,
Safe paths we tread, promises we keep.

Climbing and jumping, oh what fun,
But watch over me until the work is done.

The buggy zooms fast over paddocks of green,
Strap me in tight, so I'm safely seen.

With steady hands and a watchful eye,
We'll navigate the paths where adventures lie.

The silo stands tall with grain in its core,
Keep me from climbing to its mighty door.

Respect their height, their towering place,
Guidance and care in this open space.

The truck carries loads to places anew,
Safety means to have the clearest view.

So buckle me in on this bumpy ride,
Or keep me distant, clear on the other side.

In the shearing shed where the wool flies,
Keep me in sight, beneath watchful eyes.

Busy hands and the shearer's blade,
With care and caution, I'm unafraid.

The long grass sways with secrets beneath,
Brown snakes may lurk, in silence they sheath.

Tread with care, ever so wise,
For they lie still and hidden in nature's disguise.

Tools and machines, such fun to play,
Teach me their purpose, show me the way.

Respect and caution, lessons we learn,
Safety ensured with each careful turn.

On this farm where memories grow,
Keep me safe in the paddocks we know.

Hand in hand, in work and play,
Safe and sound in every way.

www.ingramcontent.com/pod-product-compliance
Lightning Source LLC
LaVergne TN
LVHW072111070426
835509LV00003B/119